The Navajo

by Natalie M. Rosinsky

Content Adviser: Roberta John, Navajo author,
Window Rock, Arizona

Reading Adviser: Rosemary G. Palmer, Ph.D.,
Department of Literacy, College of Education
Boise State University

COMPASS POINT BOOKS
MINNEAPOLIS, MINNESOTA

FIRST REPORTS

Compass Point Books
3109 West 50th Street, #115
Minneapolis, MN 55410

Visit Compass Point Books on the Internet at *www.compasspointbooks.com*
or e-mail your request to *custserv@compasspointbooks.com*

On the cover: Two Grey Hills rug

Photographs ©: Courtesy of Museum of Northern Arizona Photo Archives, negative no. E8952, cover; B.S.P.I./Corbis, 4; Corbis, 6–7; Nancy Carter/North Wind Picture Archives, 8–9, 15; Library of Congress, 10, 18, 23, 28; Denver Public Library, Western History Collection, photographer Ben Wittick, Call Number X-33062, 11; David Muench/Corbis, 12; Denver Public Library, Western History Collection, Call Number X-33776, 13; North Wind Picture Archives, 14; Denver Public Library, Western History Collection, photographer William M. Pennington, Call Number X-33063, 16; Pete Saloutos/Corbis, 19; Bettmann/Corbis, 20; Thomas Wiewandt/Visions of America/Corbis, 21; Kevin Fleming/Corbis, 24; Danny Lehman/Corbis, 25; Unicorn Stock Photos/John Ebeling, 27; Stock Montage, 29; Arthur Shilstone, 30–31; Time Life Pictures/Getty Images, 32–33; Denver Public Library, Western History Collection, photographer Timothy H. O'Sullivan, Call Number Z-2716, 34; Denver Public Library, Western History Collection, Call Number X-33883, 35; Denver Public Library, Western History Collection, Call Number X-33027, 36; National Archives, 37; Marilyn "Angel" Wynn, 38; AP/Wide World Photos/The Gallup Independent/Jeffery Jones, 39; Photri-Microstock/Paul Meyer, 40–41; David McNew/Getty Images, 42–43; John Cross/The Free Press, 48.

Creative Dirrector: Terri Foley
Managing Editor: Catherine Neitge
Photo Researcher: Svetlana Zhurkina
Designer/Page production: Bradfordesign, Inc./Les Tranby
Cartographer: XNR Productions, Inc.
Educational Consultant: Diane Smolinski

Library of Congress Cataloging-in-Publication Data
Rosinsky, Natalie M. (Natalie Myra)
   The Navajo / by Natalie M. Rosinsky.
     p. cm. — (First reports)
Includes bibliographical references and index.
   ISBN 0-7565-0643-3 (hardcovers)
   1. Navajo Indians—History. 2. Navajo Indians—Social life and customs. I. Title. II. Series.
   E99.N3R673 2005
979.1004'9726—dc22   2004000592

Table of Contents

*NOTE: In this book, words that are defined in the glossary are in **bold** the first time they appear in the text.*

Who Are the Navajos?

▲ *Navajo children at Canyon de Chelly, a beautiful and historic area in Arizona*

The Navajos (pronounced NAV-a-hos) are a native people of the American Southwest. Between the years 800 and 1400, historians believe their ancestors traveled there from the colder northwest coasts of Canada and Alaska. The Navajo language is like the Athabaskan languages spoken in those northern areas.

▲ *A map of past and present Navajo lands*

Today, the Navajos are the largest native tribe in the United States. (The Cherokee claim more members, but they decide membership in a different way.) There are more than 298,000 Navajos. About 174,000 of them live in the Southwest, on the Navajo **reservation** now called the Navajo Nation. This huge area of colorful deserts, canyons, and mountains is located where the states of Arizona, New Mexico, Utah, and Colorado meet. It occupies more than 25,000 square miles (65,000 square kilometers) and is about the size of West Virginia.

In their own language, the Navajos call themselves the *Diné* (pronounced deh-NEH). This Navajo word means "the people." They call their south-western homeland *Dinetah,* which means "among the people."

▲ *Beautiful Monument Valley is on the Navajo reservation in southern Utah.*

From Travelers to Farmers

▲ Ruins of the Anasazi village of Pueblo Bonito in New Mexico

The ancestors of the Navajos traveled to find food. When there was little to hunt or gather in one place, they moved to another.

When these early Navajo ancestors reached the Southwest, they found the ruins of an earlier people. The Anasazi had lived in caves and cliffs. They had grown crops and hunted near these homes.

By the time the Navajos' ancestors arrived, all the Anasazi were gone. Another group of farming people now lived in this same area. They were the Pueblo Indians. They planted and harvested corn, squash, beans, and melon. They wove baskets.

The ancestors of the Navajos traded with the Pueblo. Over time, the Navajos also learned to weave and grow crops from the Pueblo. This meeting with the Pueblo had changed their lives. They became farmers themselves.

The word Navajo even comes from the Pueblo language and means "planters of huge fields."

Unlike the hardened clay, or adobe,

△ A 1906 photo by Edward S. Curtis shows Navajo cornfields at Cañon del Muerto in Arizona.

houses of the Pueblo people who lived in this area, the Navajos built their permanent homes out of logs covered with mud. The houses were round or eight-sided, and they called them hogans. Inside, a hogan was one large room with a doorway and chimney.

▲ *Navajo women weave blankets near their hogan in the late 1880s.*

Spanish Explorers and Colonists

▲ Navajo paintings on the rock walls at Canyon de Chelly
show the arrival of Spanish soldiers in the 1500s.

In 1540, the Spanish explorer Francisco Vásquez de
Coronado arrived in the Southwest. He and his soldiers
hoped to find gold, but they failed. In 1598, a Spaniard

named Juan de Oñate returned to this area where the Pueblo and Navajos lived. Oñate brought settlers with herds of sheep, cows, goats, and pigs. He brought priests of the Roman Catholic religion. Oñate established and governed a large colony called New Mexico.

This colony brought many changes to the Pueblo and Navajos. They learned to raise sheep for meat and wool. They wove the wool into blankets, belts,

▲ *A Navajo herds sheep and goats.*

and rugs. Over time, raising sheep became an important **tradition** for the Navajos. So did riding horses, another animal the Spanish had brought with them.

Yet these traditions as well as other new **customs** came at a price. Spanish soldiers destroyed Indian homes. They killed Indian men and forced

△ *Spanish soldiers introduced the horse to the Navajo.*

Indian women and girls to work as slaves for the settlers. That is when Navajo women first saw the full cloth skirts and blouses of Spanish women. Later, these became part of traditional Navajo clothing.

Spanish soldiers sometimes made the Pueblo fight alongside them against the Navajos. At times, the Navajos raided Spanish settlements. Other local tribes such as the Apache also fought and raided. Sometimes, Spanish soldiers shed blood for little reason. In 1805, they killed more than 100 Navajo women and children hiding in a cave in Canyon de Chelly. This place became known as **Massacre** Cave. Such attacks were a daily danger to the Navajos.

▲ *More than 100 Navajo women and children were killed at Massacre Cave.*

▲ A Navajo mother holds her baby in a cradleboard in the early part of the 20th century.

Everyday Life

Family is an important part of Navajo tradition. In everyday life, Navajo people still introduce themselves by **clans** as well as by name. A mother's clan is most important. It affects who owns things and where people live. Belongings are handed down through the mother's clan.

In the past, a young Navajo husband and wife would build their hogan near the wife's mother. Several family hogans might come to be grouped together there. Apart from family groups, Navajos preferred to live away from others. They did not live in villages.

Men hunted deer and other animals. Women prepared and sewed animal skins into knee-high moccasins. These protected them from sharp desert plants. Navajo women also cooked and wove baskets, rugs, and blankets.

Women watched the sheep that were needed for **mutton** and wool. These important animals even affected where the Navajos lived. To give their sheep

▲ *A girl cards wool as Navajo women weave a blanket and a belt on looms in Arizona in 1892.*

▲ *A Navajo woman watches her sheep in present-day Arizona.*

enough grass to eat, many families built a second hogan in another place. In winter, they would move to this warmer, grass-filled spot. Women also planted and harvested crops. These included fruit trees as well as corn, beans, squash, and melon. Children would help with chores. Girls were proud to help watch the sheep they would someday own. Men took care of other herd animals.

Men defended their families. One head man might make important decisions for several families, but there was no leader for all the Navajos. There was no tribal government or **council.** Rules for how to behave were set by custom and beliefs.

△ *In the past, there was no one leader for all the Navajos.*

A Sacred Land

▲ *The Navajos call their homeland Dinetah.*

According to Navajo tradition, four Holy People created the world. They then created the first Navajos from ears of corn. These spirits set the

Navajos upon the sacred land they call Dinetah. Its four tall, colorful mountains are signs of the Holy People. Pieces of mountain blue **turquoise,** black **jet,** and yellow or white shell are other reminders of these powerful spirits.

The Navajos believe that the Holy People gave them special **ceremonies.** By completing the ceremonies, the Navajos honor their gods and help themselves.

Navajos have many ceremonies, and each has its own purpose.

The Enemy Way ceremony is supposed to help Navajo men and women cleanse their minds and rid their bodies of evil spirits.

The Blessing Way ceremony is conducted to purify the mind of all evil and bless the person with positive thoughts. The Kinaalda ceremony, it is said, will help girls become good, useful, and knowledge-able women.

▲ Edward S. Curtis photographed Navajos in ceremonial dress in 1904.

△ *An apprentice medicine man practices for a ceremony in his hogan.*

▲ *A Navajo man works on a sand painting.*

The Navajos believe that someone is healthy only when that person's body and mind are in balance and in harmony. Living in harmony with oneself, the land, and the Holy People is an important Navajo belief.

Ceremonies help Navajos keep and regain harmony. A medicine man called a *hataali* leads these ceremonies, which may last several hours or several days. The hataali has much knowledge that takes a lifetime to learn. He sings special prayers. Sometimes he also draws special sand paintings. Their colorful patterns often tell stories about the Holy People or Dinetah.

The four corners or directions of this sacred land are often part of a ceremony. One Navajo prayer tells how the Navajos feel about their land. They sing "Beauty before me, and beauty behind me, beauty above me, and beauty beneath me."

A ceremony or "sing" is also a time for family and friends to gather to show their support or to be healed. People may travel from many miles away. These gatherings may be for happy or sad events.

Navajo Weaving and Jewelry Making

▲ A Navajo woman weaves on a loom outside her hogan.

Navajos are famous for many crafts, especially weaving and jewelry making. Navajo women weave beautiful rugs. By tradition, a woman weaves on a **loom** placed outside her hogan. She uses yarn made from the wool of her own sheep. The pattern of each rug has a meaning or story. Zigzag lines show lightning, while diamond shapes may stand for stars. Some rugs tell about the Holy People. Others tell about the people or animals of Dinetah.

Navajo men and some women make wonderful silver jewelry. They learned this craft from the Spanish and Mexicans. Often, these items use the turquoise stones found in the Southwest. One traditional type of Navajo necklace looks like squash blossoms. Today, many Navajos weave rugs and make jewelry by hand to earn a living.

△ *Edward S. Curtis photographed a Navajo woman wearing a silver squash blossom necklace in 1904.*

▲ *Manuelito and his followers resisted U.S. settlement on their homeland.*

In 1821, Mexico became a separate country from Spain. Mexico controlled the Navajos' land until 1848, when it lost a war with the United States. Then, American soldiers, miners, and settlers moved into the area. Some Navajos fought these invaders. A Navajo warrior named Manuelito led one group of fighters.

In 1862, Indian scout Kit Carson told the Navajos
they had to leave their sacred land of Dinetah. He
had soldiers burn their homes and crops. Carson's

▲ *The Navajos were forced to make the Long Walk to Bosque Redondo in eastern New Mexico.*

soldiers cut down trees and drove herds away. The Navajos had no food. They had to surrender.

The United States government forced the Navajos to move far away from their homeland. Between 1863 and 1866, soldiers marched more than 8,000 Navajos away from Dinetah. They traveled southeast for 300 miles (480 kilometers). This painful trail began at Fort Defiance in Arizona, and ended at Bosque Redondo, near Fort Sumner, in eastern New Mexico. The Navajos had few wagons or horses. Many elders and sick Navajos died during these forced marches. Their terrible experiences are now known as the Long Walk.

At Bosque Redondo, the Navajos had to start over with few supplies. There was not enough food or shelter. They planted crops, but the crops failed. Thousands more of the Diné died from hunger and disease. Yet Navajo leaders did not give up. They continued to meet with government officials.

In 1868, a Navajo leader named Barboncito signed a **treaty** with the United States. It permitted the Diné to return to Dinetah. Barboncito explained how impor- tant this was for his people. "After we get back to our

▲ *The imprisoned Navajos built living quarters for U.S. soldiers at Bosque Redondo in 1865.*

country," he said, "it will brighten up again, and the Navajos will be as happy as the land. Black clouds will lift, and there will be plenty of rain to make the corn grow. It will grow in abundance, and we shall be happy."

▲ *Navajo weavers in western New Mexico in 1873*

Growth and Change

After the treaty of 1868, the Navajos asked for and got more of their homeland back. Settlers needed meat and wool from Navajo livestock. People enjoyed Navajo crafts. The United States government understood this. Over the years, it returned more of Dinetah to the Navajo reservation.

▲ *A Navajo silversmith in the late 19th century*

In 1923, Navajo people changed in another way. They established a more systematic form of government. The Navajo Tribal Council spoke for the Diné's rights and needs.

△ *Navajo girls, wearing tags on their clothes, arrive at a government school in Arizona in 1924.*

Some changes occurred that hurt the Navajos. Often, the U.S. government did not respect Navajo traditions. Many U.S. officials believed that Diné children should learn the white man's ways. Navajo children were forced to leave their families and live in faraway schools. They were not allowed to speak their own language and were severely punished if they did. They were even given new names! Some ran away.

In the 1930s and 1940s, another government program hurt the Navajos. They were forced to kill almost half of their sheep. Other livestock also had to be killed. The government believed this would prevent land from being overgrazed. Yet the plants and grasses that had been disappearing did not grow back as officials expected.

▲ *A Navajo family in front of their summer and winter hogans in the mid-1930s.*

The Navajos Today

△ *The flag of the Navajo Nation*

The Navajo Tribal Council, which is the Navajo Nation's government, has 110 different chapters or communities on the reservation. Its strength has helped the Navajos accomplish many of their goals.

▲ *A dance club performs at the opening of a new Navajo school in Prewitt, New Mexico.*

Many schools in Dinetah include lessons in Navajo language and traditions. Older students do not have to leave the reservation to go to school. They may attend Diné College, the first college in the United States established by Native Americans for

Native Americans. Diné College's main campus is in Tsaile, Arizona, with seven other community campuses in Arizona and New Mexico. The main college building in Tsaile is shaped like a hogan.

Many Navajos today, though, no longer live in hogans. Most hogans are used for traditional ceremonies. Some Navajos have joined different religions, such as the Native American Church, which uses a plant called peyote for healing purposes.

Some Navajo weavers and jewelry makers have started their own businesses. This way, they earn more money for their work. Other Navajos inside and

▲ *Many Navajos raise sheep, just like their ancestors did.*

outside the Navajo Nation work in many different professions and jobs. Within the Navajo Nation, though, many people still farm and raise sheep. Unemployment is a problem for the Navajos there.

There are other problems. Some Navajos disagree with a neighbor tribe, the Hopi, about the borders of their reservations. Also, there are not always enough doctors or teachers in the area.

In addition, officials of the Navajo Nation are concerned about mining. They fear that companies digging for coal or oil will damage their sacred land. These companies bring needed jobs. Yet the Navajos believe it is important to walk in harmony with the land. They hope this is possible in the future, as they continue to grow as a nation and as individuals.

▲ *School buses carry children across the vast Navajo Nation where the Navajos hold on to their traditions as they look to the future.*

Glossary

ceremonies—formal acts that mark special events or times

clans—groups of people related by blood or marriage

council—a small group of people that governs the whole group

customs—a group of people's usual way of doing things

jet—a black stone used in jewelry

loom—a machine or piece of equipment used to weave cloth

massacre—the killing of a group of harmless people

mutton—meat from sheep that is eaten by people

reservation—a large area of land set aside for Native Americans

tradition—a group of people's longtime way of doing something

treaty—an agreement between two groups of people that becomes the law for them

turquoise—a blue stone used in jewelry

Did You Know?

- The Navajo flag was the first Native American flag to fly into space. In 1995, astronaut Bernard Harris carried it aboard the space shuttle *Discovery*. He lived in the Navajo Nation as a child.

- Many Navajo stories are about how the world began. These stories often have animals as characters. The trickster Coyote is one of the most well-known.

- Navajo code talkers helped the United States Army win World War II (1939–1945). The enemy could not understand important radio messages sent using the Navajo language.

- Today, basketball and rodeos are popular in the Navajo Nation.

At a Glance

Tribal name: Diné

Divisions: 130 clans. The original four are the Towering House, One Walks Around You, Bitter Water, and Mud clans.

Past and present locations: where the states of Arizona, New Mexico, Utah, and Colorado intersect

Traditional houses: hogans

Traditional clothing materials: moccasins made of leather; full cloth skirts and blouses; woven wool ponchos; belts decorated with silver

Traditional transportation: horse and foot

Traditional food: mutton, corn, squash, beans, melon, peaches

Important Dates

800– 1400	Ancestors of the Navajos travel from Alaska and Canada to the Southwest.
1540	Spanish explorer Coronado arrives with horses.
1598	Spanish leader Oñate brings settlers and herds to establish the colony of New Mexico.
1805	Spanish soldiers kill Navajo women and children in Massacre Cave.
1863– 1866	8,000 Navajos are forced into the 300-mile (480-kilometer) Long Walk that kills many.
1868	Treaty between Navajos and U.S. government permits Navajos to return to a reservation established on their land.
1923	Navajo Tribal Council is established.
1969	Tribal Council establishes the Navajo Nation (rather than the Navajo Tribe).
1990	U.S. Congress passes a compensation bill for Navajo miners who were physically harmed by the terrible conditions of past uranium mining in the Navajo Nation.
2001	President George W. Bush awards gold medals to the 29 original Navajo code talkers; silver medals are awarded to all the World War II code talkers.

Want to Know More?

At the Library

Cooper, Michael L. *Indian School: Teaching the White Man's Way.*
New York: Clarion Books, 1999.

Hucko, Bruce. *A Rainbow at Night: The World in Words and Pictures
by Navajo Children.* San Francisco: Chronicle Books, 1996.

Roessel, Monty. *Songs from the Loom: A Navajo Girl Learns to
Weave.* Minneapolis: Lerner, 1995.

On the Web

For more information on the Navajos, use FactHound to track down
Web sites related to this book.

1. Go to *www.facthound.com*
2. Type in a search word related to this
   book or this book ID: 0756506433.
3. Click on the *Fetch It* button.

Your trusty FactHound will fetch the best Web sites for you!

On the Road

Canyon de Chelly National Monument
Box 588
Chinle, AZ 86503
928/674–5500
To see the remains of ancient Indian villages and visit a museum
about local tribes

National Museum of the American Indian on the National Mall
Fourth Street and Independence Avenue Southwest
Washington, DC 20560
202/287-2020
To learn about the history and culture of Native Americans at this
Smithsonian Institution museum

Index

About the Author

Natalie M. Rosinsky writes about history, social studies, economics, science, and other fun things. One of her two cats usually sits on her computer as she works in Mankato, Minnesota. Natalie earned graduate degrees from the University of Wisconsin and has been a high school and college teacher.